To : Bennett McCamley

Thank you for your safety presentation to Nova Gas Transmission in Spruce Grove, Alberta on November 10, 1998. We hope you enjoy your stay in Canada.

David Bindra.

Bhindra

ETERNAL ROCKIES

May the beauty that is the Rockies remain with you in your Dreams

ETERNAL ROCKIES

Text and Photographs by
GEORGE BRYBYCIN

giant rock tumbled down from the summit of Mt. Hector in Banff National Park, smashing itself to gravel on the western walls, ledges and benches: a loud, scary and violent event to witness in this tranquil and seemingly lifeless environment.

Lifeless? Maybe at first glance... I have seen a band of mountain goats on these western walls, and even as 1 watched, a pair of golden eagles were soaring overhead. Perhaps they know that a rockslide might mean a dead goat and a big meal.

In twenty-five years, I have been on this splendid summit four times and never noticed any visible changes. Such a period is not even an eye-blink in the millions of years of the Rockies' geological history.

When I gaze over these endless vistas, shapes and geological formations, I certainly wonder at their longevity, their indestructible appearance. If anything could seem eternal, it would be these majestic and mighty mountains.These wondrous mountains spark many philosophical and hypothetical questions, like: how high was Mt. Hector (11135/3394m) 100 million years ago? In theory, it could have been anywhere from fifty to two hundred kilometers high. Or it might have been a small hill, or even a valley. While such speculations may go unanswered, the questions themselves are as natural as the mountains.The lofty, jagged peaks of the Rockies get smaller by two to three millimeters each year, due to climatic erosion.

Since the birth of the Rockies over 100 million years ago, many violent and turbulent events have reshaped the mountains. Ten million years ago, another series of crackings, foldings and upliftings pushed the Rockies skyward again. The whole region was in restless turmoil for a very long period of time.

As recently as 12,000 years ago, during the Wisconsin glaciation, the solid ice cap pushing southward swept valleys and lower mountains, reshaping the land again. In places where the glacier dug deep and wide, large lakes formed after the glacier retreated north. One of these lakes is the pearl of today's Rockies - Lake Louise.

How will the Rockies look in 100 million years? Will they even still exist? Far too many factors will influence the region in the future, making it impossible to tell. Chances are that, millions of years from now, the Rockies will resemble today's foothills while today's foothills vanish, gradually blending in with the prairies. Lakes like the Louise will be long since gone, filled by debris and sediment carried by water from nearby heights.

If the world as we know it can survive for another 100 million years (and if Parks Canada doesn't sell the land to developers,) perhaps Homo Sapiens will manage to strike and maintain a healthy balance with the wilderness and its animals.
However, another possibility does exist. With no high mountains to catch rain producing clouds, the whole region could become an arid desert, supporting very little life.

We all like the idea of eternity, but the Rockies will one day cease to exist - worn down by erosions, earthquakes and time.

For now, however, let us have the romantic notion that the Rockies are indeed eternal and invulnerable, and that these lofty giants will please, thrill and give joy to humankind forever.

It is assumed that, for thousands of years, the Native American peoples did not climb the mountains for sport or pleasure. It took the newly arrived and adventurous Europeans of the 19th century to risk their lives by challenging the heights. At first, they were labeled as "mad dogs" for pursuing such "ungentlemanly" or "unladylike" pleasures. After Philip S. Abbot lost his life in the first climbing accident (on Mt. Lefroy in 1896), the general public proclaimed climbing to be a mindless madness.

When the railroad crossed the Rockies on its journey to the Pacific, more adventurers and Swiss mountain guides had arrived. Before long, mountaineering became a popular and acceptable thing to do. Climbing attracted people of higher education and social status.

By the end of the nineteenth century, many first ascents had been made, including Mts Temple, Victoria, Lefroy, Hector, Athabasca, Snow Dome and Diadem, to mention only those few major peaks of more than 11000/3353m elevation.

The most prominent climbing pioneers of this period were: P. S. Abbot, S. E. Allen, G. P Baker, A. P Coleman, J. N. Collie, A. S. Cyr, W. S. Drewry, C. E. Fay, J. W. A. Hickson, J. J. McArthur, C. L. Noyes, J. Outram, J. Pollinger, P. Sarbach, J. H. Scattergood, L. B. Stewart, H. E. M. Stutfield, E. Whymper, W. D. Wilcox and H. Woolley.

By 1938, all but three major peaks over 11000' had been climbed. "The unclimbable" Mt. Alberta resisted all assaults on its vertical walls until finally vanquished by a Japanese team in 1925.

Some of the most prominent people of this era were: E. Cromwell, G. Englehard, V. A. Fynn, K. Gardiner, L. Gest, L. Grassi, W. R. Hainsworht, G. B. Kinney, A. L. Mumm, A. J. Ostheimer, K. Prescott, W. B. Putnam, M. Schnellbacher, M. M. Strumia, J. M. Thorington and E. O. Wheeler.

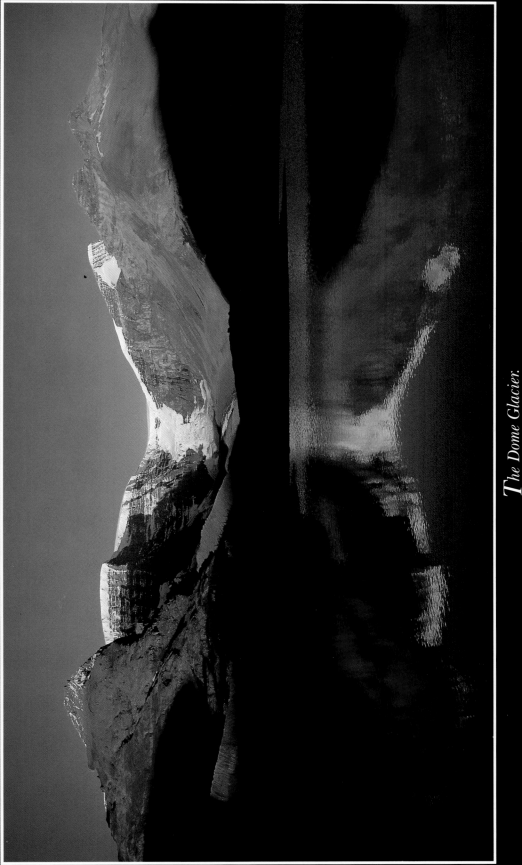

The Dome Glacier:

Engelmann Spruce and golden larch forest adorns the picturesque Cerulean Lake. Mt. Assiniboine Provincial Park.

*Heartwarming golden larches along the trail from Lake Magog to Wonder Pass.
Mt. Assiniboine Provincial Park.*

15

One of the more spectacular "must see" places of the Rockies - Peyto Lake. These emerald waters originate at the Wapta Icefield and are, in turn, the origin of the Mistaya River. Banff National Park.

Lower Waterfowl Lake, Mistaya River, Chephren Lake (above), Howse Peak (3289 m) on the left and Mt. Chephren (3265 m) comprise this peaceful autumn morning scene. Banff National Park.

The vicinity of Banff has its ambience and gentle beauty. An evening stroll along Vermilion Lakes rewards one with a perfect reflection of Mt. Rundle and the moon.

Left upper: Traffic lights on the Trans-Canada Highway against the wintry Three Sisters (2936 m) near Canmore.

Left lower: The picturesque railway town of Field, lights on the Trans-Canada Highway and Mt. Stephen (3199 m). Yoho National Park.

The mysterious and moody morning at Moraine Lake, a mountain jewel of unmatched beauty and fame. Banff National Park.

Right: Injured during the battles of rutting season, bull Elk (*Cervus canadensis*) must recover quickly before the coming of cold, harsh winter or face certain death.

Healthy green forest along the Bow River and distant Storm Mtn (3161 m) photographed on a hazy summer morning. Banff National Park.

Left: These ewes and young Bighorn Sheep (Ovis canadensis) appear contented and happy and face the winter with cautious optimism.

The gate to heaven or hell, depending on the weather. A splendid, heavenly morning on the summit of Mt. Daly (3152 m). Mt. Balfour (3272 m) dominates the Waputik Icefield and Daly Glacier (left). Crossing this place in winter white-out conditions is a very perilous journey. Yoho National Park.

The Bighorn Sheep (Ovis canadensis) is quite a resilient and adaptable animal which is doing well facing the ever expanding bulldozer civilization. In national parks or outside, sheep survive well if left alone. The one thing no animal can outwit is a bullet. Don't we all wish that trophy hunting would be abolished for good? Sometimes, when one meets the fearful and intelligent eyes of an animal, one gets the feeling that it thinks of us as the very bad and destructive animals.

The only rain forest in the entire Rocky Mountains sprawls around Mt. Robson (3954 m). The height of the giant catches the moisture coming from the Pacific, causing huge rain and snowfalls. Rich and diverse flora and fauna flourish in the area as a result. Mt. Robson Provincial Park.

Left upper: Sparkling morning dew adorns the beauty of the humble Wild Rose (Rosa woodsii).

Left lower: The delicate, intricate beauty of nature. Moss Campion (Silene acaulis).

Located 8 km northeast of Lake Louise, Mt. Richardson (3086 m) is a splendid lookout, providing many great vistas. This impressive view is to the northwest, with Mt. Hector on the right. Banff National Park.

Climbing Mt. Richardson (3086 m) is always very rewarding. The summit offer great vistas, glaciation, and the variety of alpine elements expected from a high mountain. This is the view to the northeast. Banff National Park.

Fifteen years ago, this was a pristine valley with only one gravel road. Look closely. Can you see any changes? Kananaskis Valley viewed from the summit of Mt. Kidd (2958 m).

The one and only Banff Springs Hotel. A world renowned hotel at its best. Its charm, Victorian ambience, modern services are combined with a location very few others can match. Starry skies and Sulphur Mountain (2450 m) crown the splendor of this wintry scene.

Blessed with a moist and mild climate, the Mt. Robson area enjoys rich flora and fauna. Being the highest mountain in the Canadian Rockies, Mt. Robson (3954 m) draws tourists and climbers from around the world. Mt. Robson Provincial Park.

Dramatic light highlights the Valley of the Ten Peaks. Hidden Moraine Lake and the surrounding area are major destinations for tourist, hiker and advanced climber. Banff National Park.

These weary but happy British climbers are reaching the Abbot Pass Hut where they will have a well-deserved, nice cup of tea. Illuminated by the early morning sun is hanging upper glacier of Mt. Victoria (3464 m). Banff National Park.

Only high mountains such as Mt. Temple (3543 m) can provide splendid vistas of such magnitude. On the left is Mt. Lefroy obscuring part of Mt. Victoria. A realm of snow, ice and rock. Banff National Park.

The full moon illuminates the snowy slopes of Crowfoot Mtn (3063 m) by Bow Lake, Banff National Park.

A nocturnal image of Castle Mtn (2766 m) and the Bow River under a full moon. Banff National Park.

35

Along the trail to Helen Lake and Dolomite Pass. A great display of the rich variety of mountain flowers that can be viewed here in August. The area also has abundant fauna. Banff National Park. Right: Wild Rose (Rosa woodsii) hips.

The Tower of Babel (2360 m) on the left, is located just of Moraine Lake. Several climbing routes on a fine quartzite are quite popular due to easy access and shortness of climbs. Banff National Park. Left: Autumn leaves.

Emerald waters at their best. Glacier-fed Upper Consolation Lake is located just south of Moraine Lake. This green jewel is flanked from the east by Panorama Ridge (in photo), from the south by Mt. Quadra and from the west by Mt. Babel. Banff National Park.

Nestled high up on the slopes of Mt. Temple, in the upper part of Paradise Valley - Lake Annette is a true emerald jewel amongst Rocky Mountain waters. Golden larch trees are at their best in late September and early October. Banff National Park.

The awesome beauty of the heights commands respect, fear and admiration. Mt. Hungabee (3493 m) on the left and Mt. Biddle (3319 m) viewed from Odaray Mtn (3159 m). Yoho National Park. Wouldn't you rather climb a mountain?

41

Surveying the beautiful but perilous mountain world from Pyramid Mtn (2766 m) looking southwest, Jasper National Park. Why do people climb mountain? Children climb trees, walls, anything. Fearless youngsters climb just for the challenge of it: "I can do it and you can't!" A few years later and it becomes a habit. Some of the reasons we climb are the sport's physical aspects, the technical inclinations and sheer competitive spirit. Climbing builds strong character, mind and body. However, it is an exquisite but a bit dangerous sport so… do it carefully.

The west part of the Wapta Icefield guarded by the splendid sentinel, Mt. Baker (3172 m) on the right. Many mountaineering, climbing and ski routes crisscross this very attractive and challenging area. Photographed on a crisp autumn morning from Mistaya Mtn (3095 m), Banff National Park.

43

A snowy windswept Mt. Daly (3152 m) extends its "warm" hospitality to a lone, bivouacking climber. A splendid panorama unfolds to the southwest. Major recognizable peaks, from the left: Mts Stephen, Vaux, Wapta, King, Niles and the President. Yoho National Park.

A young bull Elk (Cervus elaphus) faces the grim reality of six months of coming winter. If snowfall is abundant and temperatures very low, many animals will not survive the long, harsh winter.

Left upper: A Rock Ptarmigan (Lagopus mutus) can afford only three dresses a year: brown in the summer, gray in the autumn and pure white for winter.

Left lower: Canada Goose (Branta canadensis) is the most common of fourteen species of geese.

A mountain paradise of great magnitude. The first morning light illuminates Mt. Balfour (3272 m) and the peaks of Waputik and Wapta Icefields. In the shadows the still waters of Hector Lake partially mirror the scene. The only drawback is the direct sunlight which washes it out and flattens a bit. Photographed from Mt. Hector (3394 m) Banff National Park.

47

The unmatched beauty of the Mt. Assiniboine area photographed from Sundance Range, looking west. On the left stands Mt. Gloria (2908 m), Mt. Aye (3243 m) in the centre and Mt. Assiniboine (3618 m) with Lunette Peak (3400 m) to the left of Mt. Assiniboine. Marvel Lake must certainly marvel at its surroundings - beautiful forest, the other lakes and these beautiful mountains all around it; not to mention a few resident grizzly bears. Banff National Park.

It could be called a mountain paradise, a spectacular wilderness or God's country as seen from the summit of Mt. Hector (3394 m). The gorgeous emerald Hector Lake, the lush green Bow Valley and the endless vistas of the majestic Rockies, Banff National Park.

On the way down from Abbot Pass to Lake O'Hara. A short stop at Lake Oesa, a place of extraordinary beauty and charm but at the same time rugged, wild and dangerous. The possibility of a rock or ice avalanche is ever present. Yoho National Park.

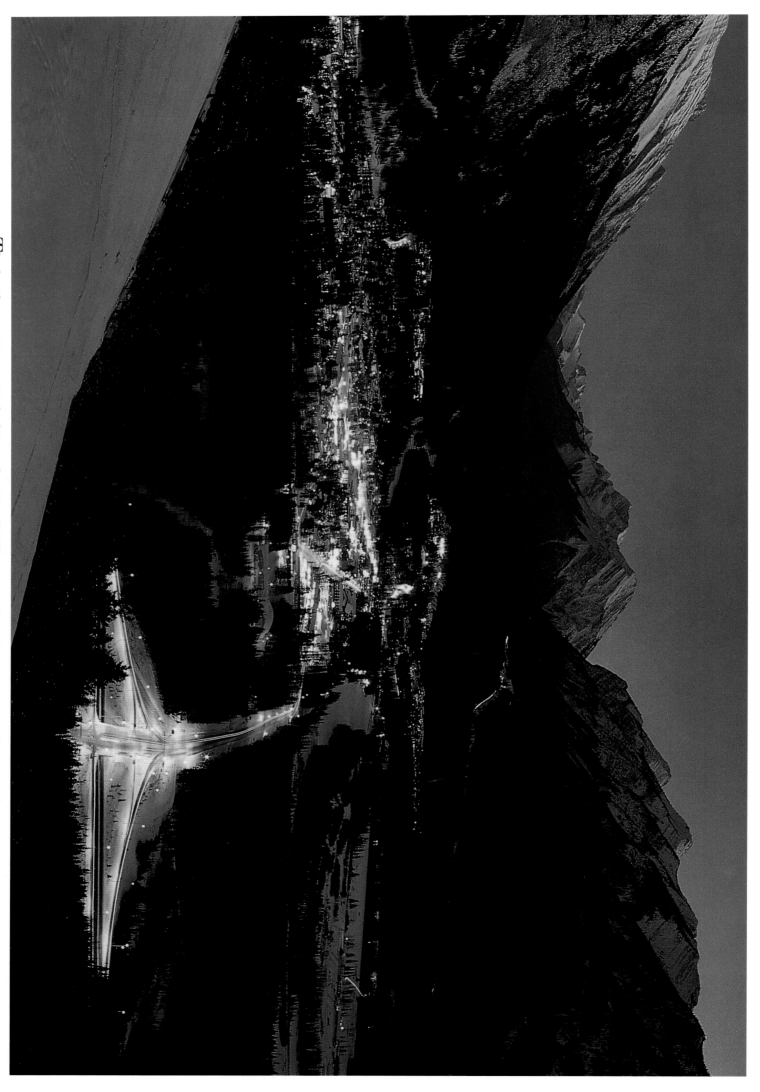

The bustling winter capital of Canada - Banff, Alberta. A first-class resort to visit at any time, year round. Banff has world-class hotels, gourmet restaurants and fine shopping for all tastes and needs. Three major ski areas in the vicinity provide the world's best powder snow and truly spectacular skiing!

A picture tells the truth. Banff is superb, spectacular and charming. Viewed from Cascade Mtn (2998 m)
The sprawling year-round mountain resort is nestled between Mt. Rundle, Sulphur Mtn and Cascade
Mtn at an elevation of 1380 m/4530'. The impressive ranges to the south are dominated
by the pointed Canadian Matterhorn - Mt. Assiniboine (3618 m).

Heart-leaved Arnica (*Arnica cordifolia*).

Glacier Lily (*Erythronium grandiflorum*).

Willow leaves (genus *salix*).

Pearly Everlasting (*Anaphalis margaritacea*) and Western Red Maple.

52

The Valley of the Ten Peaks. Banff National Park. On the way to climb the east face of Mt. Temple (3543 m) on a fine autumn morning - exactly one hundred years after S. E. S. Allen, L. F. Frissel and W. D. Wilcox first ascended the mountain in 1894 via a "tourist route" from Sentinel Pass.

The ultimate wilderness. The Ramparts and Amethyst Lake at Tonquin Valley. Jasper National Park. Regardless of some human presence, the valley is pristine and ecologically healthy. A small herd of Mountain Caribou (Rangifer tarandus montanus) survive in the company of moose, grizzly bears, wolves and a number of smaller animals. The area can be accessed from Cavell Road or Marmot Road via Maccarib Pass. It was here, by Portal Creek, that a camper was killed and partially eaten by a starving grizzly bear in 1992.

Mountain Goat (Oreamnos americanus) nanny and kid overlooking Athabasca River. Jasper National Park. Ornery by nature, goats are territorial and frequently battle over favorite pastures.

A small mountain tarn along a Wonder Pass trail, the distant Nub Peak (2748 m) and golden larches create this serene and inspiring autumn image. Mt. Assiniboine Provincial Park.

An autumn view from The Nublet. Mt. Assiniboine Provincial Park. From the left is Lake Magog, Sunburst Lake and Cerulean Lake; all flanked by Mt. Magog (3095 m) on the left, Mt. Assiniboine (3618 m), Sunburst Peak (2820 m) and The Marshal (3190 m). The extraordinary beauty of this area amply warrants incorporation into Kootenay National Park, thus stopping a serious abuse of fragile nature.

Witnessing nature's spectacle from the summit of Mt.Carthew (2621 m). Waterton Lakes National Park. At the centre is Mt. Alderson with the Montana Rockies beyond.

Left: There are four glaciers on Mt. Robson (3954 m). Some are small bodies of ice but Robson Glacier is 7 km long. This photo features Berg Glacier on the north face, tumbling down into Berg Lake. Mt. Robson Provincial Park.

Bow Lake as photographed from Bow Peak. Banff National Park.

North face of Mt. Robson (3954 m) and Berg Lake. Mt. Robson Prov. Park.

60

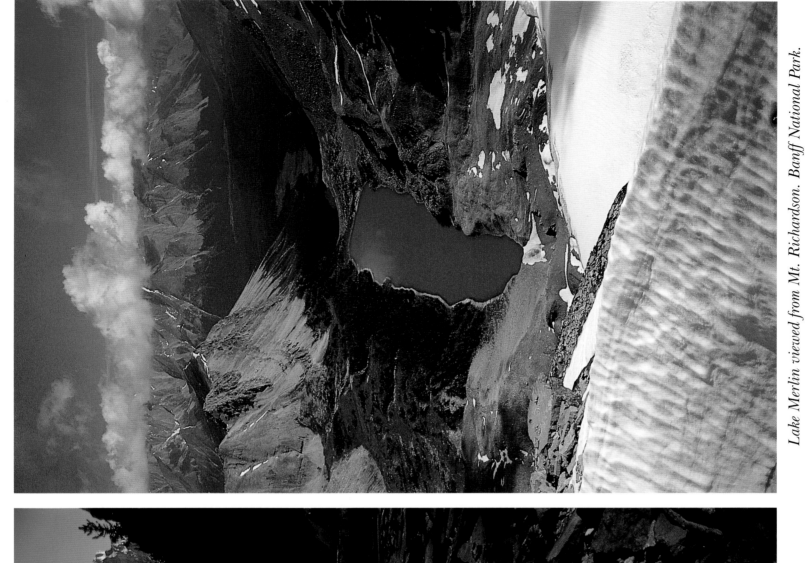

Lake Merlin viewed from Mt. Richardson. Banff National Park.

Mt. Huber (3368 m) and Mary Lake. Yoho National Park.

Located southwest of Lake Louise, Paradise Valley lives up to its name. Many natural wonders can be seen along Paradise Creek trails. The prominent one is Giant Steps - a system of cascading rapids and falls on Paradise Creek, whose pure, clear waters originate from Horseshoe and other glaciers along the great divide's sky high mountains. Banff National Park.

Well known for its clear emerald waters and splendid surroundings, Emerald Lake is a major tourist destination. Mt. Burgess (2599 m) is a known landmark of Yoho National Park. Existing facilities and heavy use of the area raises concerns about balancing tourism and the role and aims of national parks - keeping it pristine.

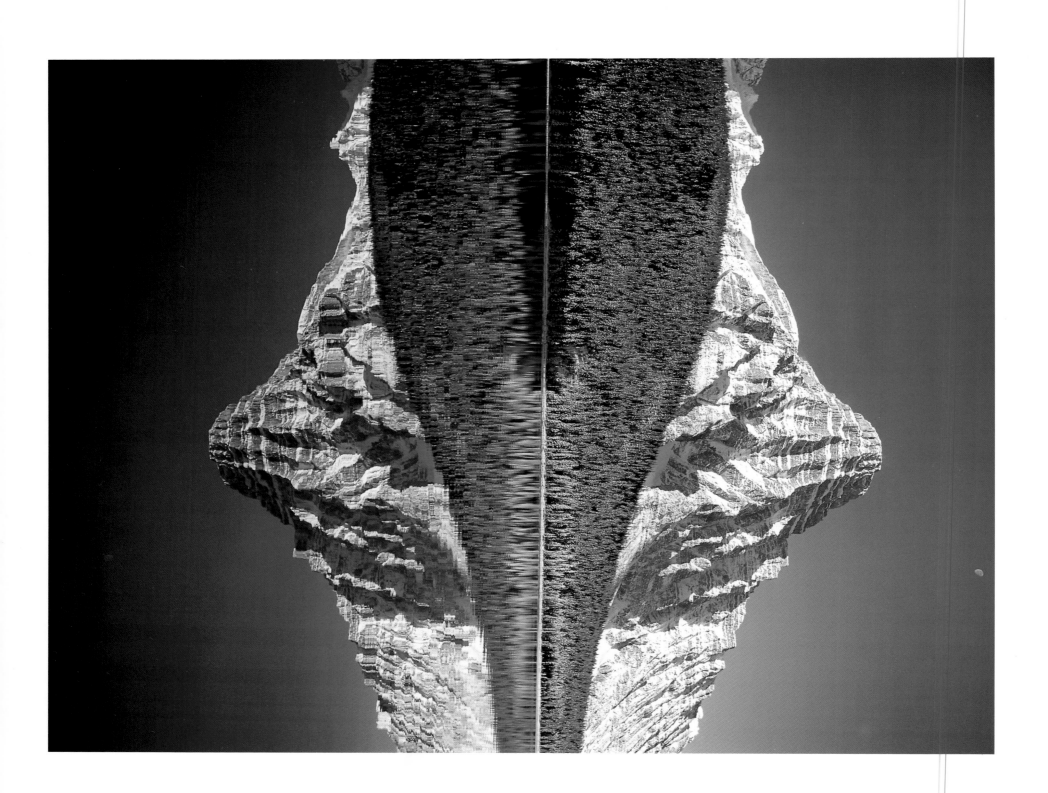

The annual "festival of colours" at Larch Valley above Moraine Lake. Banff National Park. Some of the "Ten Peaks" provide splendid alpine background.

Left: Lower Waterfowl Lake is known for its serenity and beauty. A moose and waterfowl habitat surrounded by great high mountains and dusted by the first autumn snow. Mt. Chephren (3266 m) stands tall above the crystalline lake. Banff National Park.

One of the world's greatest hotels - Chateau Lake Louise in the stillness of early winter evening: reflected in the beautiful Lake Louise and guarded by majestic Mt. Richardson (3086 m). A place to visit and enjoy year round. Banff National Park.

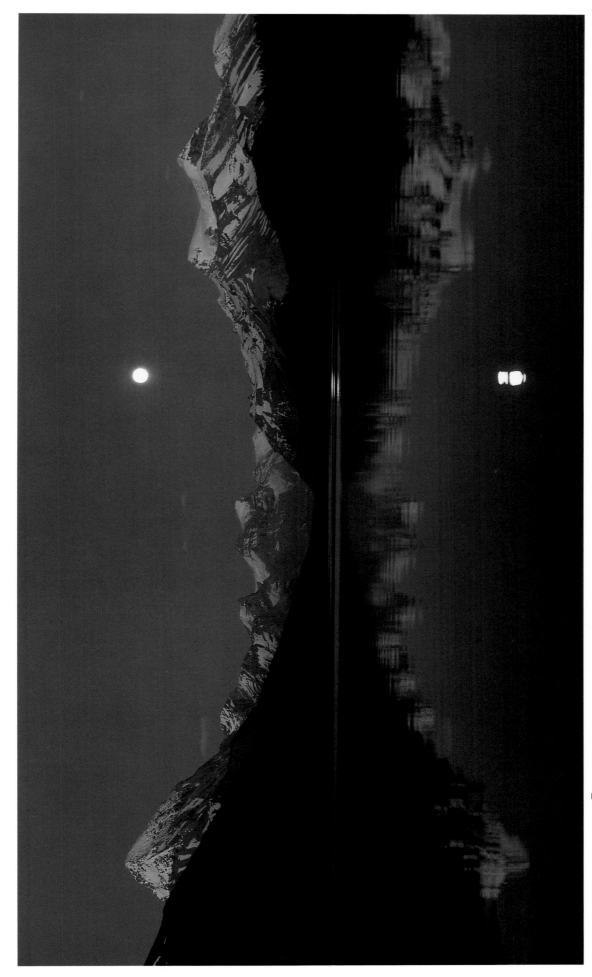

Like a honeymoon scene from a romantic movie, Maligne Lake shines under a full moon on a summer night. The area is a true gem of unspoiled wilderness. The flora shows tundra characteristics due to the northern latitude and high elevation, while the fauna is very rich. Jasper National Park.

Elk or Wapiti (*Cervus canadensis*).

Black Bear (*Ursus americanus*).

Grizzly Bear (*Ursus arctos*).

Bighorn Sheep (*Ovis canadensis*).

68

Not many North American animals can match the size, strength and majesty of the Moose (Alces alces), the world's largest deer. Still quite common in the north and in national parks but almost eliminated in areas where rifle-wielding humans live.

The North Star, or Polaris, accompanied by millions of "circling" stars high above the wintry Castle Mtn (2766 m). A nocturnal rhapsody in black. Banff National Park.

A half-hour interval time exposure of the moon "travelling" across the wintry skies in an exquisite company of twinkling stars. A moonlight sonata. Banff National Park.

A summer holiday on Mt. Edith Cavell (3362 m). Jasper National Park.

This way down. Couloir 3 - 4 above Moraine Lake. Banff National Park.

72

Descending Victoria Glacier through "The Death Trap". Banff N. P.

Climbing the glaciated Mt. Lefroy (3423 m) from Abbot Pass. Banff N. P.

How clear can a mountain lake be? It can be so clear that one can see every single rock, boulder, log or twig five meters deep on the lake's bottom. Now that is the clear, clean water of green Lower Consolation Lake. Banff National Park.

The serenity and peace of this morning at Patricia Lake, Jasper National Park, brings back the words of a great mountaineer of long ago, Conrad Kain: "I think myself fortunate amidst the peace and quiet of nature."

Elizabeth Parker Hut, located near Lake O'Hara. Yoho National Park.

76

Lawrence Grassi Hut, located on Cummins Ridge by Clemenceau Icefield.

Abbot Pass Hut, located between Mt. Lefroy and Mt. Victoria. Banff/Yoho National Parks.

Skoki Lodge, located in Skoki Valley. Banff National Park.

The spacious and modern Bow Hut is located east of Bow Glacier by the Wapta Icefield. Banff National Park. It seems that a ghost of the author appears in the foreground of this half-hour time exposure photo.

77

A small mountain tarn along Lake O'Hara to Lake Oesa trail. Glacier and Ringrose Peaks in the background. Yoho National Park. In spite of protective national park status, the Lake O'Hara area is heavily used and thus abused. Definitely, a more stringent entry quota system is required.

In many areas outside our national parks, there is hardly any pristine wilderness left. Logging and mining do most of the destruction. Some people say: "I love nature so much that I bought an off-road vehicle just to get closer to it." The scars the tires of these vehicles leave on mountain meadows, will be there for 60 years. If a few other "nature lovers" follow these tracks, a road is created that will last forever. If you really love nature, just walk along the hiking trails. Kananaskis Valley, Fireweed (Epilobium angustifolium) and Opal Range.

On the peak (2745 m) of Slate Range just east of Baker Lake. A sharp eye will pick out the recognizable mountains looking north, from the left: Fossil, Hector, Skoki, Molar, Cyclone, Pipestone, Oyster and Mt. Drummond with its glaciers. Banff National Park.

On Fossil Mtn (2946 m) looking southeast, green Baker Lake below. Tilted, Brachiopod and Little Baker Lakes in the centre. To the left is Baker Creek Valley and Wildflower Creek, leading to flowery Pulsatilla Pass. Banff National Park.

The picturesque Herbert Lake located just northwest of Lake Louise. The peaks of Bow Range with Mt. Niblock (2976 m) in the centre, reflected in these mirror-like waters. Banff National Park.

The magic of twilight over Maligne Lake. Jasper National Park. A fabulous place of extraordinary beauty, pristine wilderness and rich fauna. Only very limited human activities are allowed here to protect a very fragile northern wilderness.

Venus's Slipper (Calypso bulbosa).

Shooting Star (Dodecatheon pauciflorum).

Yellow Lady's Slipper (Cypripedium calceolus).

Western Wood Lily (Lilium montanum).

84

The monarch of the northern wilderness: the mighty Grizzly Bear (Ursus arctos). The coloration of this omnivorous predator ranges from light tawn, to brown, to deep reddish. There is much confusion as which bears belong to which of the seven groups of bears. The largest of the so-called "dish-faced bears" is Alaska's Kodiak (Ursus arctos middendorffi). Some say the grizzly is merely a regional variation, in colour and size, of a Kodiak.

To take this picture, the author had to spend a winter night on the summit of Mt. Bourgeau (2930 m), just west of Banff. The crisp morning brought a temperature of -27° C and a splendid sunrise. How cold and tough was it? Well, I quickly took a few photos and even more quickly jumped back into my sleeping bag! Mt. Assiniboine graces the horizon on the right. Banff National Park.

The great mountain panorama viewed from Sundance Range, looking west. On the left is Owl Lake, on the right, Marvel Lake. Above Owl Lake is Mt. Aurora (2790 m). Between the lakes is Marvel Peak (2658 m). The sharp peak is Mt. Gloria (2908 m) then Mt. Aye (3243 m), and Lunette Peak (3400 m) a southern hump of Assiniboine, and Mt. Assiniboine (3618 m). Banff National Park.

The snowy summit of Mt. Edith Cavell (3362 m) and its lower northwest peak are perfectly reflected in crystal clear Cavell Lake. A Japanese proverb states: "You are a fool if you don't climb Mt. Fuji, but you are a bigger fool if you climb it twice." Would George qualify for the mega-fool title after climbing Mt. Cavell four times?

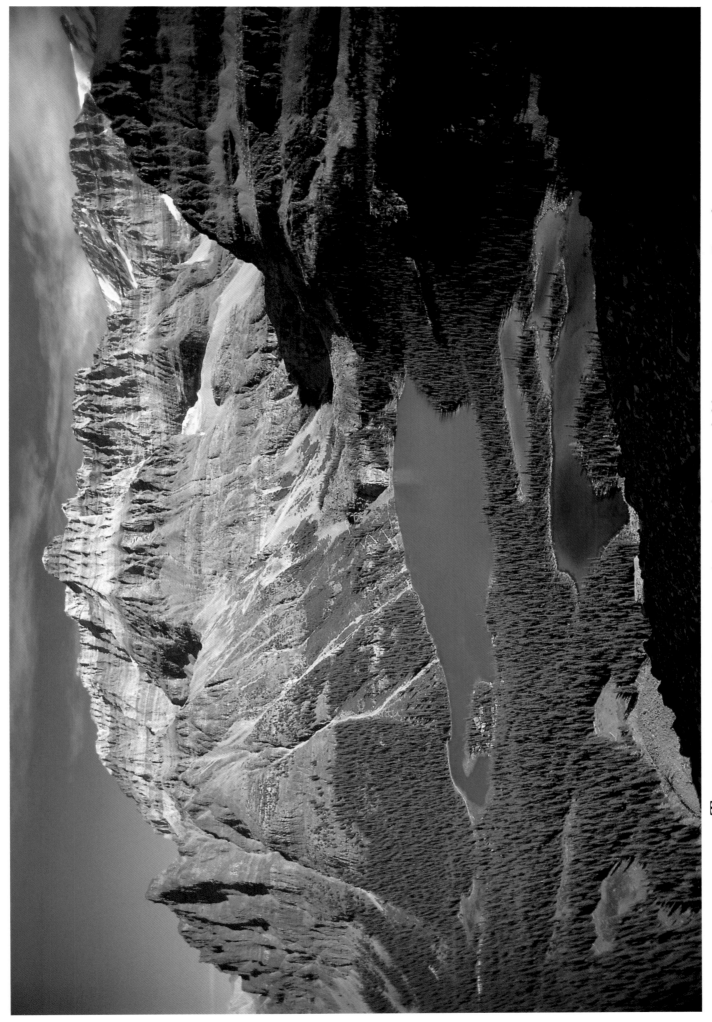

The splendid area of Lake O'Hara and Mary Lake, surrounded by majestic mountains. From the left: Wiwaxy Peaks (2703 m), Mt. Victoria (3464 m), Mt. Huber (3368 m), Mt. Lefroy (3423 m) and Yukness Mtn (2847 m), all viewed from Mt. Schaffer (2692 m). Yoho National Park. The magnetism of the area attracts many visitors. Will more restrictions be needed to protect the fragile environment?

Approaching the summit of Mt. Temple (3543 m). An immense panorama to the southwest: some of the "Ten Peaks" in the foreground; Vermilion Range in the middle ground and the Bugaboos on the horizon. A great, fun place to visit - why don't you give it a try? Banff National Park.

A real feast for the eyes, heart and soul but a real pain for the body. It is a strong, nearly spiritual experience to wonder at an act of creation of this magnitude. Looking south from Mt. Temple (3543 m) at Moraine Lake and approximately fifty different mountains. Banff National Park.

A short northern summer has exploded in the bright colours of Fireweed (Epilobium angustifolium) at Bow Summit. Banff National Park. Above the timberline, where the summer may be less than five months long, the vegetation barely manages to reproduce its cycle, yet the beauty and lushness of nature is astonishingly rich. It was here on Bow Summit that a grizzly bear mother with a cub, charged and nearly made a meal of the author, before hibernating in late October. The same lady, photographed two years earlier (page 85), was quite well-behaved and minded her own business.

Dramatic light creates a dramatic picture. The north glacier of Mt. Hector in the foreground; in the middle is twin-peak Molar Mtn (3022 m); the horizon is dominated by massive Cataract Peak (3333 m). A cold and rugged, but fascinating high altitude world. Banff National Park.

A late autumn image of Mt. Robson (3954 m), the highest mountain in the Canadian Rockies. Beginning in 1908, many unsuccessful attempts have been made on these formidable walls. Finally, in 1913, Conrad Kain led fellow climbers W. W. Foster and A. H. MacCarthy on the first successful ascent to this splendid but perilous summit. Mt. Robson Provincial Park.

Located between The Snow Dome (3456 m) and Mt. Kitchener (3505 m), the Dome Glacier is one of the smaller ice tongues of the Columbia Icefield. Nearly four kilometers long, half of it is hidden under gravel and rock debris. Numerous hidden crevasses and icefalls cause climbers to avoid it as a route up to the Icefield. Jasper National Park.

One may visit a lake ten times and never see the same colour, light or mood. Perhaps plain blue skies may be good enough for a postcard, but real photos should feature mood, ambience, colour and, perhaps, still water to allow reflections. Lake Louise. Banff National Park.

Here is a moody photo. Heavy overcast with soft light - a shaft of light lit these flowers for just a moment. Do not hesitate to photograph even in adverse light conditions. You never know what and how the camera and film will see things. The Valley of the Ten Peaks. Banff National Park.

The elusive Aurora Borealis which are not easy to capture on film. This photograph was taken in the northern part of Banff National Park.

Bivouacking on the slopes of Odaray Mtn (3159 m). High peaks of the Bow Range, from Mt. Victoria to Hungabee Mtn can be seen. In the centre is Lake O'Hara. Yoho National Park.

One can only hope that this boulder won't move, at least not at night. On the slopes of Mt. Hector (3394 m). Banff National Park.

Left upper: Camping on the lower slopes of The Snow Dome (3456 m) allowed this crisp, clear photo to be taken … twenty-two years ago. Basking in the morning sun is the second-highest mountain in the Canadian Rockies Mt. Columbia (3747 m). Jasper National Park.

Left lower: Nearing the north face of Mt. Joffre (3450 m). Kananaskis Country. The summit attempt was aborted due to hurricane strength winds. This is a three-day climb involving a 23 km walk one way, mostly through moon-like terrain, and the elevation gain is 1730 m.

The north side of glaciated Observation Peak (3174 m), located north of Bow Summit. The ice-capped giant on the right is Mt. Hector (3394.) Banff National Park.

A classic from the author's photo library: an early morning haze swaddling the peaks and valleys from Kananaskis to Mt. Assiniboine. Photographed from Storm Mtn (3161 m). Banff National Park.

103

Everything appears smaller and flat when a fish-eye lens is used because it covers such a huge area. Here the summit cornice and southwest ridge of Mt. Temple (3543 m) is featured in a pleasant sunrise that is dressed up by the use of a red filter. Banff National Park.

Along Sunwapta River by the Columbia Icefield. The Endless Chain Range is on the horizon. It had been raining heavily and, suddenly, the magic sky started turning redder and redder. This strong colour is seldom seen in the mountains. No filter. Jasper National Park.

The joy of mountaineering. Who said that mountains are cold and in-hospitable place? Just look at this happy frostbitten and swollen face!

It all started on a crisp, sunny winter morning on the Jasper Highway near Peyto Lake. The target: a four day Wapta Icefield traverse. On the left: passing by the icefalls on Peyto Peak's east slopes. On the right: two photos from the trip. Banff National Park. A target is one thing - the realization of it is another. It seems that the elements and natural hazards are not merely items in information centre brochures. They really do exist and can be very hazardous to your health, or even life. For the full story on five days in hell, read on page 9.

Approaching High Balfour Col.

Digging into Scott Duncan Hut.

The crystalline blue waters of Maligne Lake and an unmatched panorama of wild mountains, healthy green forests and clear air. This is the most spectacular part of Jasper National Park.

Between Lake Oesa and Lake O'Hara, there are a few cascades and waterfalls. Water from small glaciers and snowfields runs down the slopes, making this almost desolate rocky valley inhabitable. Notably, a healthy band of goats can be seen here year round. A wide range of rodents also make their homes here. Marmot and wolverines may be seen and a martin often visits Abbot Hut. Yoho National Park.

113

Bunchberry (Cornus canadensis).

Yellow Columbine (Aquilegia flavescens).

Emerald Lake is a major tourist attraction in Yoho National Park. The beautiful environment, with its rich flora and fauna make the area a popular visiting spot.

September weather is dry and clouds are a rarity. Local ground moisture evaporates and forms clouds in the valleys overnight but the morning sun burns them off quickly. Mt. Chephren (3265 m) on the left and White Pyramid (3276 m) are draped by a fancy, white morning veil. Banff National Park.

The same circumstances as in the photo opposite, have created these clouds over Kicking Horse River Valley, near Field. Yoho National Park. The sharp, white peak on the right is Mt. King (2892 m) and was first ascended in 1892 by remarkable solo climber and adventurer, J. J. McArthur.

The upper part of Paradise Valley, just south of Lake Louise. Banff National Park. For millions of years, rock falls from Mt. Temple and other peaks filled the valley. Golden larches stand against the wall of Mt. Lefroy, left and the gentle eastern slopes of Mt. Aberdeen.

A very attractive panorama unfolds from the summit of Mt. Whymper (2845 m) to the south. To the left is the great, snowy dome of Mt. Ball (3311 m), while Stanley Peak (3155 m) is next and the endless peaks of Vermilion Range are on the right. Kootenay National Park.

Fay Hut, Prospectors Valley, Kootenay National Park.

Whyte Hut above Peyto Glacier, Banff National Park.

Brewster Cabin near Shadow Lake, Banff National Park.

Naiset Cabins by Lake Magog, Mt. Assiniboine Provincial Park.

*A few hundred cross-country skiers run for fun, fame or glory in the annual race staged
in March at Lake Louise. Banff National Park. Would you participate?
It's healthy, entertaining and great fun!*

A short northern summer has finally arrived, to the joy of the Elk (Cervus canadensis) and all wildlife. They must build up their body-fat quickly to sustain them through soon approaching long winter. Jasper National Park.

The intricate, gentle beauty of the Common Harebell (Campanula rotundifolia). A Ladybug (Family coccinellidae) finds this stem a hospitable place to take a nap. Both are common throughout the Rockies.

Starry, starry night... If Beethoven were to be reincarnated and spend a few nights at Lake Louise, it would almost certainly inspire a "Moonlight Sonata II." Fairview Mtn (2745 m) and Lake Louise lit by a half moon. Banff National Park.

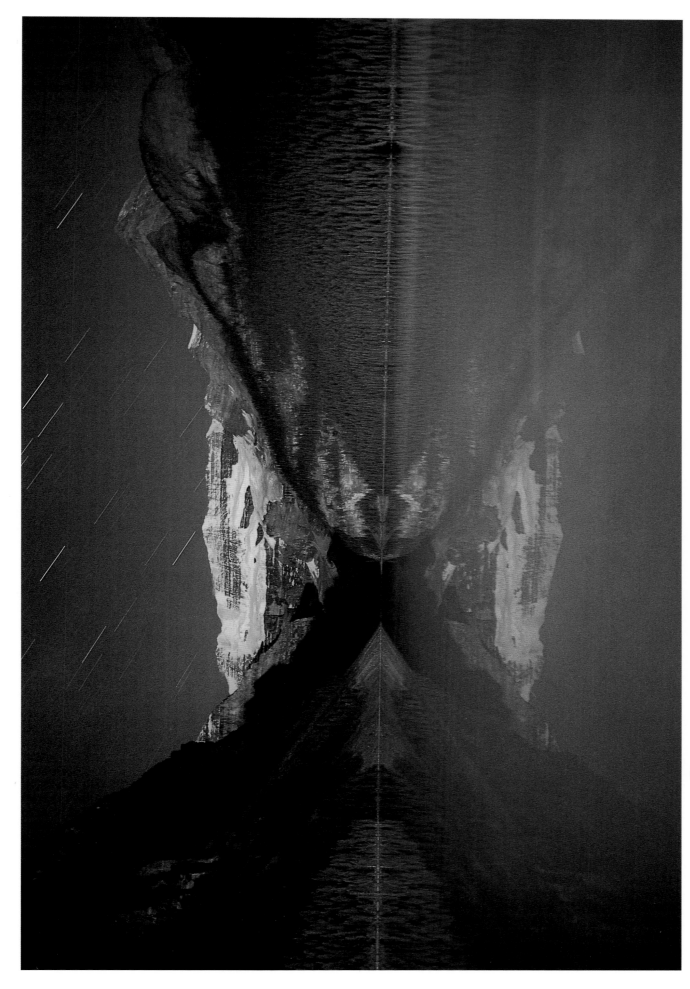

Blue moon... or green moon? If George Gershwin had spent a few nights by Lake Louise, we would probably be listening to "Rhapsody in Green." The author shot several night frames in different seasons and got all sorts of different colours. Mt. Victoria (3464 m) and Lake Louise. Banff National Park.

Flowers are the joy of mountain meadows: a showcase of wildness, a paradise for naturalists and photographers, though these are merely its human terms. In nature, the real role of flowers is to provide birds with seeds, insects with nectar and pollen and grazers with protein - for them, it is a food source. The best time to see these flowers, depending on the area, is early July to early August. For spring flowers, it would be in May or June. The Willow-Herb (Epilobium latifolium) on Quartz Hill, Banff National Park.

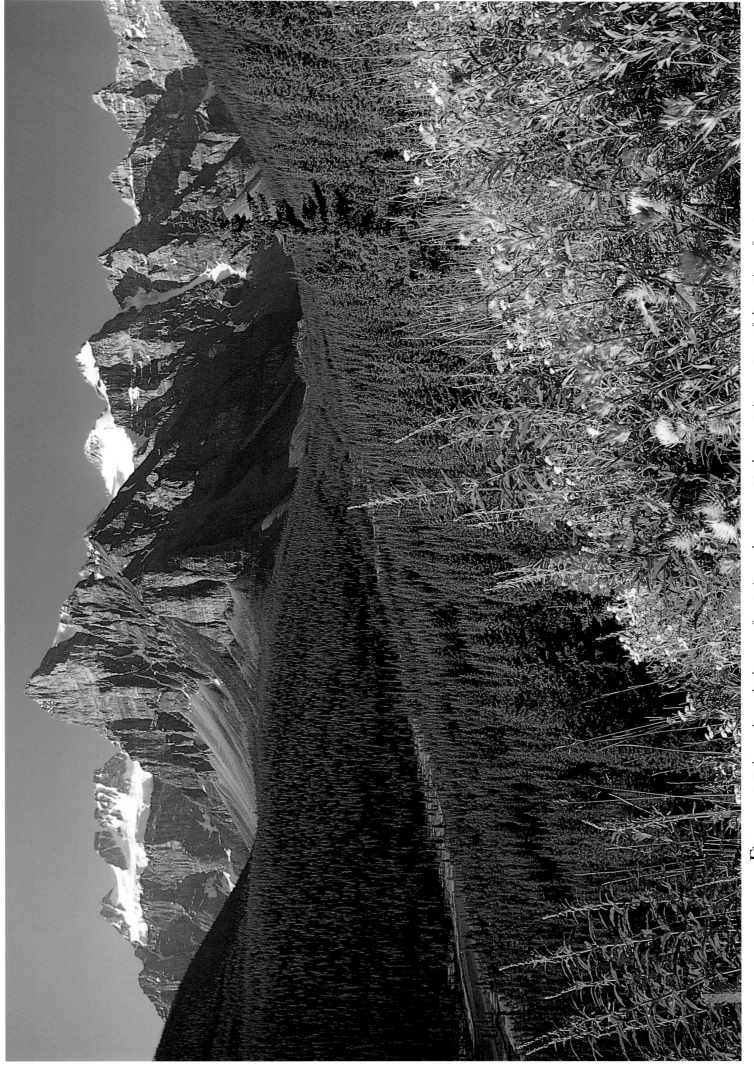

Flower-carpeted meadows, lush green forest, jagged, snow capped mountains - a powerful creation of nature and a realm of beauty, inspiration and peace. The Valley of the Ten Peaks. Banff National Park.

*A perfect morning reflection of House Peak (3289 m) and surrounding mountains in
Upper Waterfowl Lake. Home for numerous waterfowl and a healthy moose
population. Banff National Park.*

Left upper: Lower Waterfowl Lake and reflection of Mt. Chephren. Banff National Park.

Left lower: Lower Consolation Lake and the reflection of Mt. Babel. Banff National Park.

Sunrise and moonset over Mt. Victoria (3464 m). Banff National Park. This natural phenomenon occurs every month but, because of weather conditions, it is very difficult to capture it on film. Do you go to the mountains? Do you enjoy their company? Hiking through the woods is so inspiring, pleasant and healthy. It invigorates and cleanses your body and mind. Mountains are like good friends, in whose company one can walk, talk or just listen to the whisper, song or roar of the heights. Listen to the music of the Eternal Rockies.

ENVIRONMENTAL THOUGHTS AND MORE ...

Blessed with great wisdom, our forefathers created one of the world's finest national park system in the Canadian Rockies. Their idea was to protect the pristine wild areas; leaving them undisturbed for the enjoyment of all future generations.

How have we honored this wise and noble concept these several generations later?

Rapid population growth and the devastation people can bring, is clearly evident in the Rockies. Increasing traffic through the parks kills hundreds of animals every year. Some flowers have become extinct in the more heavily used areas of the parks because of illegal flower picking. The majestic moose have been eliminated from the busy areas of Banff National Park.

The grizzly bear is seldom seen: eagles, falcons and ospreys are rare sights. The only species which is flourishing is homo sapiens, which can be seen commonly and is mostly associated with litter, garbage, noise and pollution.

If national parks cannot protect the flora and fauna of these beautiful natural areas, who or what will?

When driving west toward Banff, one can see a "scenic" cement plant and the huge scars left on the mountain side after rock removal. These scars are several kilometers long, reaching almost to the park's boundary and will irritate the eyes of the parks visitors forever.

In the west, on the doorsteps of the national parks, clear-cut logging of the spectacular ancient forests continues shamelessly. The devastation of the landscape is indescribable and the consequences frightening. The creatures that inhabit the dense forests are having their homes destroyed or are being killed outright. Soil losses caused by erosion, floods and landslides are a direct result of clear-cut logging.

The concerned and considerate people who protest against this senseless destruction are unceremoniously thrown in jail as common criminals. So much for democracy and the protection of the superb natural areas of British Columbia and Alberta.

There should be at least a five kilometer belt of protected land surrounding all national parks.. where hunting, fishing, logging, mining and major development would be strictly forbidden. Instead, at the eastern boundary of Banff National Park, a large town exists and is growing at an alarming rate. Even worse, the ever hungry developers plan to triple the town's size - build large hotels, a number of golf courses and create lots of traffic. This will cause a lot of pollution and, again, dislodge the original inhabitants - the wild animals.

Do we want a pristine wilderness or noisy amusement parks with casinos, carousels and popcorn? We can't have it both ways! Will people come from large, noisy, polluted cities to holiday in exactly the same kind of hell?

Unfortunately, there is more bad news than good. One early summer day as I drove along Jasper Highway, I noticed garbage, left from winter, all along the road. I was very irritated by the way people break the law in regard to littering in our parks. Intimidating as it was, I decided to clean up after someone else. Over a stretch of 30 km, I picked up over 300 large pieces of trash. It was tiring, but very satisfying to see that one side of the road was now spotless. I hoped someone would do the other side. We should be able to expect park staff to catch and heavily fine litterers. It is disgraceful to see the scenic roads through our world famous parks littered so badly. Why not show a bit more pride in our parks. Why not show some respect and demonstrate a higher personal culture. Always have a small garbage can or trash bag in your car - then use it.

There are other sad stories, too. Once, after climbing, while I rested in my car in the parking lot, I saw eight people picking flowers in just one hour. I informed them that they were breaking park law and that they would be fined $100 if a park warden should catch them. Six people told me they were unaware that picking flowers was prohibited. The other two gave me cold looks, picked more flowers and walked away. They all knew they were in a national park.

The illogical act of picking flowers puzzles me the most. Why would a person who is hundreds of kilometers from home, on a hot summer day, want to pick flowers that will die in five minutes? What is the idea here? Not only is the act irrational and stupid, it is also illegal. Flowers need to ripen in order to reproduce and others would appreciate seeing them, so please - don't mindlessly pick them,

Along Banff's Vermilion Lake, I have watched a family of six throw rocks at waterfowl and squirrels. My lecture had no effect on any of them, so I drove into Banff and reported them to a warden.

While on my way to a climb in Yoho, I heard a persistent hammering. I looked up to see a guy hammering away at some fossils on the slope. He bragged that his backpack was full of great stuff. I ran down to inform the warden and the barbarian was caught and prosecuted.

Throwing rocks into streams and lakes continues to be a favorite pastime in the parks. Kids, adults, whole families join in the "fun". It is silly, rowdy behavior and against park rules. If everyone did it, the lakes would disappear - filled by rocks. Please think. Do not do it.

I often see vehicles driving off the road to camp illegally in the parks. People cut down trees, build fires and leave garbage behind.

I am saddened and disturbed by this type of behavior, either in the parks or any wilderness area. In every case I try to get involved to try to protect our parks. In one case, however, I ran into four very large, drunk gentlemen with axes camping illegally. I bid them good day and ran for my life. Things like this make me heartsick.

Far too many people haven't got the slightest idea about what national parks are for. Or, they just don't care! How can we reach and educate them? It seems to be an impossible, futile task. People who exhibit no respect, admiration and appreciation for nature's beauty and healing power cannot be reached. The only language they will understand is the harsh implementation of the law. Talking softly and giving warnings simply won't do - a big stick will. A $500 fine will educate anyone. Clearly, we need more park wardens if our parks are to survive and these fines could pay their wages.

Hunting is something I do not even want to talk about.

However, since we do not have a protective zone around our national parks, hunters stand two feet outside the park's boundary and wait for tame park game to come out so they can kill it. If you're in the wrong spot, you can get shot, too. I fail to understand the logic behind hunting. If you eat a steak once a day for a year, it will cost you about $1600. There is no economic sense to spending thousands of dollars on hunting equipment, licence, truck and gas just to kill one or two animals. I guess these people just love to hunt, so perhaps I should stop here, before someone mistakes me for a moose. Bless you, gents.

In our ever shrinking world, environmental concerns should be paramount among global matters. We should declare the entire Rocky Mountain area to be one giant national park but the world's heavy industry produces enough pollution to contaminate the whole planet. The pollution rises to the stratosphere to return, mostly, as acid rain.

It is currently fashionable to blame Brazil for the wanton destruction of tropical rain forest and rightly so. However, let's remember that the U.S. had eliminated most of its forests over a century ago and Canada is rapidly catching up. Less than 20% of the land in Western Europe is forested but a hundred years ago, the percentage was more like 60%. Japan is still 50% forest because it buys all of its lumber abroad.

The overpopulated China has virtually no forests of any kind and continues to build more environment polluting heavy industry, while their population runs wildly out of control. At the same time, most tropical countries, Canada and Scandinavia pollute very little and produce the bulk of clean air on this planet. We cannot blame arid Saudi Arabia or Libya for not growing lush forests, but must blame industrial countries for polluting the world while using other countries' clean

air. Environmental equilibrium must be found. All should, and must contribute to a "global clean air bank." Highly developed countries must green up their own devastated areas, practice more environmentally friendly ways to manufacture and not force others to breathe their ugly and damaging pollution.

Life cannot be sustained without trees and oxygen: green lands are more precious than we want to realize. One tree absorbs about 4.5 kg. of carbon monoxide a year. That's why we feel so great after a weekend hike in the wilderness, or so rotten after living in a large city for a long time. We all need a green tonic of wilderness exposure to live a healthy, worthwhile life. So, since we need to cut trees for lumber, we should be planting billions of trees in their place.

One old and not so wise habit should be eliminated: the habit of buying Christmas trees. Although we all love a Christmas tree, thanks to Christmas commercial hysteria, we waste five hundred million trees a year worldwide.

Wouldn't it be wise to break such a wasteful habit and be more considerate... to ourselves? Buy a plastic tree, it will last forever and cost less, too.

Every country in the world, where climate permits, must set the goal to have 10 - 15% of its area given over to green national parks and plant lots of trees in their cities as well as in the countryside: along roads, railway tracks, rivers and so on. There is easily room for twenty times the number of trees we have now. If Western Europe, India and California, among others, weren't so totally deforested, they would not suffer so many devastating floods and would save billions of dollars.

Look at your own property. There is likely room to plant one or several trees. You could have your own miniature forest with trees, squirrels and birds. It would give you cool, soothing shade on hot days, provide fruit, clean polluted air and please your senses with eye catching beauty and delightful fragrances. Have you ever had a good look at any tree? Whether an oak, fir, cedar or palm tree, it is a beautiful and powerful creation of nature.

Speaking of the global ecology, Taiwan has learned its lesson about what modern pollution does to people. To rectify their severe problems, the Taiwanese have designated 15% of their country's land for green national parks.

Canada and Poland are two more examples of good global citizenship - recently each has created three new parks, and plan to do more.

Here, for the first time, I would like to share with you, my little green secret. There was an ugly gravel pit in the Rockies, a real eyesore that was left after road construction. Since the soil was poor and there was little water available, I figured it would be a grey treeless pit forever. Then, I had an idea. I plant trees there every spring - dozens of willows and poplars. The survival rate was poor. 4 in 10 trees survived, but I have persisted and now there is a healthy little grove of green trees on that spot. Its presence will help other plants to grow in its shadows. I know that nature, with a little help, will reclaim this devastated area completely.

International environmental actions and laws have effectively stopped the slaughter of baby seals and the ivory trade is almost eradicated. Hopefully, no decent person will ever buy an ivory product because it spells the death of majestic elephants and fascinating rhinos. Adult seals could be hunted in a reasonable amount.

They provide meat, soap, clothing and many other things for northern aboriginals who only hunt for what they need to survive. Seals also take too many of the scarce fish that we could certainly use.

The disturbing trend of buying certain parts of some animals, like bears, still goes on. Some people buy these items in the mistaken belief that they will increase their vitality and sexual potency as well as having other medical properties. There is absolutely no scientific evidence to support these contentions! They are a myth, a superstitious leftover from legends of witchcraft in the dark ages. It is highly disturbing that allegedly intelligent, civilized people ravage the world's bear population for such a misguided reason. Most buyers of these items are orientals from countries that have runaway population explosions. Do they really need more sexual stimulation? What's wrong with this picture? Aren't we trying to reduce the world's overpopulation and poverty?

Presently we manage to eat up most of the fish in the oceans. Some species of fish are nearly extinct, with no hope of recovery. Commercially speaking, the Atlantic Northern Cod was declared extinct in 1995. Other species will soon follow. Doesn't this tell us anything? This small planet of ours is filled to capacity and we are already killing each other just for some living space and food.

The only solution to this problem is to reduce the population - have only one child, or none.

Here my belief clashes head on with the Vatican official policy which promotes the ancient and outdated idea: "be fruitful, multiply and populate the Earth." Why doesn't the Holy See realize that our little planet has reached the ecological meltdown point with nearly six billion inhabitants (1995). Nearly a billion people live in misery, starving and dying of malnutrition - which should be a clear indicator to the Vatican to take a more modern stand on the population issue.

The greenhouse effect, global warming, the damaged ozone layer - what are we doing about the daily bad news spawned by these things? Most of us do nothing. Life just goes on - the very life that created these problems. The low lands of Bangladesh, the Netherlands, or Venice will slowly submerge. The more

damage to the environment, the faster the submerging. Is it too late to do anything but take swimming lessons? We could stop the trend and reverse the damage but knowing the human character, with its greed and vanity, makes it seem unlikely.

We continue to build houses with single pane windows; we leave the car running for half an hour. Large office buildings often have one master light switch and when the cleaners work until midnight, the whole building is lit. We set our thermostats at 22°C forever and trot off to work, or go on vacation, leaving the furnace working overtime to pollute the atmosphere. Is it the cheap energy, or just a lack of thought, or both? Wouldn't it be wise to pass laws to regulate all that and hire government inspectors to enforce them? Government? Enforcing anything? There is a new trend developing - a small, powerless government providing no help, services or protection for ordinary people and privatizing everything. The official reason for this is to cut down the deficit. The rich, with their armies of lawyers, would be able to do whatever they pleased. They would be the law and the government. Can we afford to let that happen?

There is a variety of accommodation in the Rocky Mountain Resorts: hotels, motels, hostels. Too many of these are poorly managed. Many of them have doors and windows that are so sloppily fitted that I estimate 25% of their heat escapes. I have seen a bathroom 12 m. square that was lit by five lightbulbs when one or two would have been enough and dens lit by 40 bulbs. The light is "on" everywhere, day and night. Waste, waste! Large hotels tend to be the worst offenders. In the winter many of their doors and windows are wide open, many of which are broken and cannot be closed. This means 20 - 30% more money is spent on heating and this cost is passed on to the customer. No wonder the price of accommodations is sky high. And what about wasted energy and the pollution it causes?

The attitude seems to be: "who cares?" Perhaps some sloppy, lazy managers should be fired.

The apartment buildings where I used to live went through a new manager every few months. A lazy, careless one would be fired and the next one would be worse. Outside lights were left 'on' twenty-four hours a day. Hall windows were left wide open in the winter, even when the temperature dropped to -40°C and the heat was left on in the hottest parts of the summer. Not only did these irresponsible people cause rents to go up, they also caused pollution by wasting energy.

Perhaps you will recall the news story about the aspiring actress who needed twelve towels to dry herself after a bath in a California hotel. Why? Maybe she thought she was a queen? I sincerely hope that even real queens use only one towel after they bathe. Since I am not a king, I use the same towel three or four times and when on vacation, I instruct the maid to leave my wet towel to dry and be reused. After all, we are clean after a bath and we only need the towel to dry ourselves. Washing towels (2000 per day in a large hotel - 2012 if a queen stays there) needs detergent, highly toxic bleach, water and energy which spells a lot of ugly pollution. Following my example and not the California queen's, that pollution could be cut by at least a third.

People frequently toss a single tissue into the toilet and flush it away with gallons of precious water. What a mindless waste! Use a garbage can. It costs 40 cents to make a gallon of water drinkable.

I would also like to touch briefly on the environmental aspects of some consumer products. Disposable products should not be allowed. They should be banned once and for all. Give me one reason why not. Once used, a huge, non-biodegradable diaper goes into the garbage. Plastic disposable cameras cannot be reloaded and flashlights are useless when their built-in batteries die. Guess where they go. What a waste! Please, do not buy disposable products. If we all don't buy them they will be discontinued. Many products are packaged in large boxes which are half empty, sometimes 70% empty. I have never seen a box 100% full of any product. What a waste of trees and cardboard. The government could simply order the manufacturers to fill the boxes properly but doesn't seem to do something which so clearly makes sense. Never buy really cheap items: they soon break and require replacing. They may cost 99 cents, but stores sell millions of them and soon they all go to the sanitary landfill and cause huge amounts of pollution. Cheap is expensive. Pay more for quality products that last many times longer. Avoid eateries where disposable dishes and cutlery are used. Refuse straws, or lids on your drinks. These amount to several million a day worldwide. Instead of drinking a thirst-causing, chemical-filled pop, have a nice healthy glass of water, milk or fruit juice. It is cool to be smart. Companies that spend 25% of their budget on advertising will, most likely, not have enough money to produce a quality product.

If you read lifestyle advertising as being just the opposite of what they are saying, you will be pretty close to the reality of the situation.

I would like to move a bit off the topic, if I may, to say a few things to young people. For youngsters, everything is fine, cool, great and no problem. Optimistic by nature, as they should be, young people truly believe that they are invincible and immortal, and that nothing bad will ever happen to them. Realistically, young people die tragically every day. It is unfortunate that it is only when we reach middle age that we see what the system, the establishment, has done to us while we were young and vulnerable.

All the lifestyle advertising that tells us that this is "in", or that is "out"; you "must" have this, or you are a nobody - all of this is manufactured by cynical adults who are taking advantage of you. When some "wizard" of fashion tells you what is

"in" to wear, give them a Trudeau salute and wear what is right for you. Tidy and clean is good enough, especially when you are young and have little money. You might not think you are gullible and naïve, but you are if you cave in to the lures of addictive products. Booze, coffee and cigarette ads shamelessly promote products that have been proved to be harmful. They are addictive drugs just like cocaine and heroine. You may be tempted to try these things, experiment a bit, but be aware of the high price to be paid if you make any mistakes.

You can always experiment safely with three different fruit juices, but not with cocaine, crack and heroin. Some substances are so potent and addictive that one exposure will hook you for good. If you, in your youth, need an outside substance to "get happy", then there is something very wrong in your life and drugs won't make it better. If you say life is boring, you haven't been trying very hard. Get into sports, music, art. Climb a mountain, join the Scouts, help others. Be considerate and caring, become an environmentalist - this poor, old planet needs all the help she can get. You live here so see what you can do to make it a better place. You have a voice!

You can continue your education and be straight, smart, healthy and happy. You can become a positive person and contribute or, you can drop out of school and become a drifter, an addict, lose your health, fry your brain and die in a dumpster. In today's increasingly technological world, you cannot function without an education. What will you do if you drop out of school? Deliver pizza? Work in a warehouse for the rest of your life? Are these your life's ambitions?

I speak from experience. My best friend in high school decided he had had enough. He started drinking and smoking right in class and was expelled immediately. His father, a court justice, his family and friends all tried to save him, but to no avail. The rebel, he knew better. He held odd jobs and drifted around, and soon enough, he got in trouble with the law.

His misery did not last for very long. One day he was found on a park bench, drunk and frozen to death. What a senseless waste of a life that could have been so beautiful. His father died two months later of a broken heart and his mother literally lost her mind soon after.

We all have choices to make. Make yours on the right side of the "stupid line."

There are more deadly environmental nightmares brewing right now in Eastern Europe, Russia and China. Since the collapse of communism, money hungry capitalists are working overtime building fast food outlets, dog food outlets and commercial joints on every corner. What will be sold there? Mostly cheap third class products destined for a quick trip to the garbage dump. Guns, drugs, pornography and prostitution are now openly available to... destroy the very fabric of their societies. Also available are disposable products, triplepackaging and plastic, plastic,

plastic. All this is hyped by useless advertising papers which waste ever more trees. I hope these people will reject that invasion of the unscrupulous, valueless "money culture".

At this rate, the forests of Siberia will disappear before an environmental program can take off in Russia. If the same thing happens in China, world pollution will increase by 25% and that will be irreparable. The ozone layer will never rebuild itself.

Western societies condemn and fight tobacco smoking as deadly and thus unacceptable and yet spend a fortune on lifestyle advertising in Eastern Europe to promote... cancer, by pushing cheap tobacco products, full of tar and nicotine, which will kill millions of people. In Russia almost everyone smokes and about 350,000 people die every year of smoking related illnesses, mostly the very painful lung and throat cancers. This is tragic and not very smart.

These people who are free at last, should be taught by the more developed west about how to live a healthy and wholesome life - instead, these gullible and novelty-hungry folks are told to buy useless, and frequently, harmful products. Anything to make a dollar! What a shame - killing people for money. How mercenary. What values and morals are these? What about the governments in these eastern countries? Are they already too corrupt to do the right thing? Why don't they ban all alcohol and tobacco advertising and raise the legal age of consumption for these harmful substances to nineteen or twenty? By that age, most people are way too smart to start habits that may kill them. Wake up people!

Look now, at the unfolding Dutch tragedy. After centuries of existence, this small, remarkable country is facing an ecological disaster that is not of its own making. As the greenhouse effect melts the polar ice caps, the oceans rise, threatening almost half of Holland with submerging. From the south, a heavily industrialized neighbor causes severe air, soil and water contamination.

All biological life, including man, is threatened. The Dutch have no alternative but to drink the undrinkable toxic water of the Rhine. That water also contaminated a large coastal area 30 km deep into the North Sea. By now, most industrialized countries have done the same damage to at least some of their rivers and coastal waters.

Let's remember that heavy industry, chemical and nuclear power production have only been around for about 60 years. What horrifying damage they have done in that very short time. What is the reason that whales are dying in Alaska and Patagonia, so far from human population and industry? The oceans are dying. Why is the snow on Mt. Everest so contaminated? Because the world is dying. Russia dumps its nuclear and industrial waste into polar regions and we correctly blame them for that. But what do we do with our wastes? Do we eat them? As long as the population, industry and consumption grow, more damage to the environment will follow. Will people come to their senses and stop demanding "more, more?" No. Greed and materialism have become more deeply rooted than reason and logic. Far too many people sincerely, but incorrectly, believe that the more stuff they own, the better off they are. The greed mentality is a product of a system whose only value is "MORE! MORE!"

What really counts is who you are; what your values, morals and principles are - not how much stuff you own.

Great, positive people who contribute to society, humanity, the world, are philanthropists, altruists who have big hearts, great minds and noble intentions. Money has nothing to do with it.

The "more, more,"syndrome causes more production, more consumption, more pollution. This quickens the destruction of our health, our lives, our environment and finally, our planet. Make your choice and be sure it is a wise one. If you make the wrong choice here are some of the consequences to be expected - sooner than we care to realize! The oceans will die; the land masses will be mostly build up and paved over by 20 billion desperate people looking for living space. What then? The vital life-sustaining ecology will be eliminated. Nature's immune system, and therefore humanity's, will be no more. New diseases will develop (consider AIDS and flesh-eating bacteria to be a small warning) and wipe out most of the population. A few people will survive, here and there. Then nature will rebound and come back. Then what? People will start to populate the place more and more, and will want "more and more". The full circle will be repeated. Aren't we ugly? Dystopia? Fiction? The younger of you may have the dubious pleasure of witnessing the beginning of the end. In the meantime, we still must buy high-tech sneakers with colored lights in the heels. Isn't that cool? We can't live without it! But there's mercury in it! So what? All that counts is that people buy it! After all, we want more.

In the last 30 years, Brazil has doubled its population. What does this mean? More poverty and less education. What do the poor and uneducated do? They contribute more children, which means 240 million Brazilians in the next 25 years. That means at least 50% of the Amazon jungle will be gone. If China, Indonesia, India and a few others follow this irresponsible trend, the world's population will reach 20 billion by 2100 A.D. and that will not be a very pretty picture. Take a picture of our blue skies today, so you can show your grandchildren - they will only know grey and brown skies, like the ones seen by Chicagoans, Shanghaians and Ruhrans today.

Enough of that gray-black global tragedy. We have enough problems here in our own national parks. Have you seen anything you don't think should be in a national park? Have you seen a sign by a creek near the huge parking lot that reads

"Water polluted. Do not drink." "Polluted water in a national park? Is something very fundamentally wrong here? Are we going in a wrong direction or are we already completely lost?

Sadly it seems like every second animal in our national parks is mutilated by a tag, collar, radio transmitter or whatever. Must we know where a grizzly bear (page 68) goes for lunch or a drink, or where and with whom it sleeps? Isn't that managing, arranging and handling wildlife? Wasn't wildlife in national parks supposed to be left undisturbed, beautiful, wild and free?

Would you enjoy having yellow tags stuck in your ears for the rest of your life? Leave the wildlife alone and it will flourish as it always did long before we started interfering.

In Canada, one may still go into wilderness and see no humans all day. In Hong Kong, there are 9000 people per square mile in their wilderness. Which lifestyle would you prefer?

To protect our national parks, and whatever is left of our wilderness, when an election is called - vote an environmentalist, social worker or teacher into government. Ignore the business' tycoons and lawyers. Their track records speak for themselves.

Are you gracefully approaching the dusk of your life? Perhaps you have no idea who really deserves to be put in your will?

Here is a noble idea: will your money to a nature conservancy organization. It will be used to buy wilderness land and protect it from development. Or, you could donate your land now, with the right to live on it until you die. You will rest in peace when you leave a green legacy. A noble idea indeed.

Most of this text, on a wide range of topics, may sound gloomy, even bitter. If I had more space, I could convince you that this world is far from being perfect and thus, my writing is mostly about my concerns. Certain topics and problems must be pointed out, addressed clearly and discussed before society will notice, understand and take a stand.

I am not trying to be a moralist, do-gooder, or set the world on fire - even when I sound a bit like a catastrophist. I am just trying to express my personal, not necessarily right, opinions and concerns. I want our world to be a better place to live in for all of us.

Photographs of the Rockies show us what is at stake, what we could lose if... Make a choice, take a stand, become a warden of our wilderness, a custodian of our nature. Be a steward of a green, healthy and beautiful Canada. Oh, and do yourself a favor: plant ten or twenty trees on your property, soon. Green is beautiful, and healthy, too.

Text Editor: SHELDON WIEBE

Design: George Brybycin

Printed and bound in Singapore by

Khai Wah-Ferco Pte Ltd.

Copyright © 1995 by G B Publishing

First Edition 1995

ISBN 0-919029-23-X Hardcover

For current list, please write to:

G B PUBLISHING, Box 6292, Station D, Calgary, Alberta Canada T2P 2C9

Front cover: The Valley of the Ten Peaks, Banff National Park
Back cover: Herbert Lake, Banff National Park
Page 1 View to the west from Cascade Mtn. Banff National Park
Page 2 Broad-leaved Willow-Herb (Epilobium latifolium)
Page 3 Herbert Lake, Banff National Park
Page 4 The Valley of the Ten Peaks, Banff National Park
Page 5 Looking east from Odaray Mtn. Yoho National Park

THE AUTHOR

The extraordinary beauty of the Canadian Rocky Mountains has enchanted many creative people. George Brybycin is no exception. Brybycin has spent the last twenty-five years being driven by the vision of capturing the essence of the Rockies' intense beauty on film.

Inspired by the Rockies, Brybycin found his "just do it" personality being shaped by countless nights spent on these rugged, unforgiving mountains - in cold, rain and snow.

His many jaunts into the mountains at virtually any and every time of the year, have given George a reputation as one of the most prolific mountain photographers in Canada.

This album is a reflection of a humble, non-materialistic and very happy man. Those of his creations to be found here should lift your spirits and brighten your life. After all, they've given George creative fulfillment and that is a pretty good reason for living.